CONTENTS

Since its discovery in 1938, LSD has been the subject of many extravagant and varied claims. Proponents such as guru Timothy Leary believed that LSD could provide a mystical experience and expand the user's consciousness. By contrast, a 1968 issue of *Life* magazine stated, "An LSD trip is not always a round trip. What the LSD user may be buying is a one-way ticket to an asylum, a prison, or a grave." Researchers studied LSD as a possible cure for mental illnesses. The Central Intelligence Agency (CIA) investigated LSD as a possible mind-control drug.

To this day, many myths and misperceptions persist about LSD. Other hallucinogens have also been subject to misinformation and confusion. A government antidrug campaign released images that seemed to imply that using Ecstasy creates holes in the brain (it doesn't, although Ecstasy may cause long-term changes in the brain). A 2010 article described how some ketamine addicts became incontinent (unable to control their bladders) or needed bladder surgery as a result of long-term use (that one's true). Many sources state that hallucinogens cause psychosis. Current research indicates that hallucinogens probably do not cause psychosis. However, in people who

A single dose of 50 to 100 micrograms of LSD—less than the weight of two grains of salt—is contained on a square of blotter paper.

already have a family history of or tendency toward mental ill-ness, hallucinogens and other substances may trigger serious reactions.

Even the term "hallucinogen" represents a point of conten-tion. A true hallucination is the product of a person's mind and has no basis in reality. An LSD experience, however, alters users' perceptions of their surroundings, but it does not cause a break with reality. Users realize that the distorted visions and feelings are illusions. Alternate terms for "hallucinogen" have been proposed. The term "entheogen" emphasizes the drug's spiritual potential. The term "psychedelic" signifies that the drug is mind revealing. Nonetheless, "hallucinogen" remains the most commonly used term in most contexts. During the first half of the twentieth century, psychologists and researchers believed that hallucinogens held great potential for treating mental illness. Throughout the 1960s, recreational use of LSD and other hallucinogens became widespread. To policy makers, it was clear that the drugs were a danger to society and needed to be banned.

Only recently have researchers resumed exploring the potential medical uses of hallucinogens. These drugs are still not well understood. The fact that the medical and scientific communities are researching hallucinogens for their legitimate potential uses, however, doesn't mean that they're safe for recreational use.

1

INVENTING

LSD

LSD (lysergic acid diethylamide) is the most potent hallucinogenic drug, having a very powerful effect in very small doses. It changes a person's perceptions, emotions, and thought processes. All mind-altering drugs—whether they be stimulants, depressants, hallucinogens, or other types—work by binding to receptor sites in the brain and affecting the brain's neurochemistry. The precise mechanism behind LSD's effect on the brain is still not fully understood.

Much is misunderstood about the drug in popular opinion as well. During the 1960s, the rebellious behavior of the hippie generation was often blamed on LSD. Scientists produced dubious claims of grave long-term consequences. The assertion that LSD caused birth defects, for example, was disproved by later research. The media reported sensationalistic stories of young people being injured or even killed while under the influence. For example, nobody who took LSD was actually blinded by staring directly at the sun as was widely reported. Some users may have suffered retinal damage, but even that milder account is sometimes dismissed as a myth.

Nevertheless, because of its powerful effects on the mind, LSD should not be considered safe for recreational use. Its effects can vary greatly from one person to another. People who are emotionally fragile or have a tendency toward mental illness, in particular, should never even consider experimenting with LSD.

Hofmann's Bicycle Ride

LSD is a synthetic drug, meaning that it is manufactured in a laboratory, rather than found in nature. Lysergic acid, a precursor chemical to LSD, is found in some plants and in ergot, a fungus that grows on rye. Scientists isolated the compound in the lab in the early 1930s.

In 1938, a Swiss chemist named Albert Hofmann was researching chemicals related to lysergic acid while working for

Albert Hofmann (1906–2008) believed strongly in the therapeutic and spiritual potential of LSD, but he disapproved of heedless recreational use of the drug.

a pharmaceutical company. He isolated different derivatives of the compound and studied their medical properties. One of the derivatives he synthesized was LSD-25. The acronym "LSD" comes from the German term *Lysergsäure-diäthylamid*. Hofmann hoped that LSD-25 would prove useful in treating respiratory and circulatory problems, but tests on animals showed no promise. He set LSD-25 aside.

Hofmann was still intrigued by LSD-25, however, and he synthesized another batch in the lab in 1943. That day, he started to feel peculiar and decided to leave work early, riding his bicycle home. He found that his sense of time was distorted, and the landscape around him seemed to bend as if viewed through a curved mirror, but Hofmann made the trip home safely. He speculated that some of the chemical had been absorbed through his skin. Since LSD must be ingested, however, it's more probable that he touched his mouth with fingers that bore LSD residue. A few days later, Hoffman intentionally ingested LSD-25, taking a dosage far larger than what is now known to be effective. Once again, he experienced a hallucinatory state of strange visions and vivid colors.

After further testing, the pharmaceutical company Hoffman worked for patented LSD and began to market it under the name Delysid. It was intended to be administered as an aid to psychotherapy. LSD was first used in the United States at the Boston Psychopathic Hospital, in Massachusetts, in 1949.

Therapeutic Potential

For doctors and medical researchers, LSD represented an exciting new avenue of therapy. They wondered whether, since LSD changed people's thoughts and perceptions, it could benefit people with mental illness. Could the drug perhaps counter the ravages of diseases such as schizophrenia by altering patients' awareness? By 1965, tens of thousands of patients had been given LSD, and over two thousand papers had been written about the drug's effects. Meanwhile, the CIA and U.S. military investigated the drug's detrimental effects on the mind.

Some of the most groundbreaking research on LSD was performed in Saskatchewan, Canada, by Dr. Humphry Osmond, a psychiatrist. His subjects were given a medical

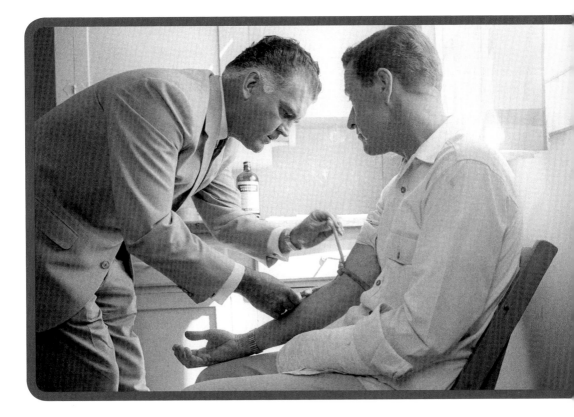

A volunteer in a 1966 LSD research project in Viejes, California, receives an injection. While some early LSD trials were medically ethical, others caused harm to the participants.

examination before the tests, and they were monitored throughout. One of Osmond's volunteers was the writer and intellectual Aldous Huxley, author of the 1932 novel *Brave New World*. Huxley wrote about his experiences with psychedelic drugs in the book *The Doors of Perception* (1954).

Osmond found that the experiences induced by LSD resembled the state of mind in people suffering from schizophrenia. He also discovered that LSD had potential to assist in the treatment of alcoholism. In one trial, patients were given a single large dose of LSD on the theory that it could produce a transformative experience similar to when some alcoholics "hit bottom" and change their habits. Within a year, 50 percent of the patients were still sober after LSD treatment—a high rate of success compared to other treatments for alcoholism. LSD was also found to relieve the suffering of terminally ill patients.

In 1959, LSD was discussed in an international conference chaired by Dr. Paul Hoch, who had worked for the CIA and the U.S. Army. Hoch was contemptuous of the idea that LSD had therapeutic value, dismissing it as an "essentially anxiety-producing drug." This view was to become the official position of the U.S. government.

Dropping Acid

One of the early proponents of LSD as a transformative agent was Al Hubbard, sometimes called the "Johnny Appleseed of LSD" for his promotion of the drug. Hubbard was acquainted with Dr. Humphry Osmond. Unlike Osmond, however, Hubbard was not only interested in LSD's therapeutic uses, but also its mystical and creative potential.

In 1960, psychologist and Harvard professor Timothy Leary began studying the effects of psychedelic drugs. He lost his position at Harvard in 1963 and became an advocate of LSD and the transcendent experience it induced. Leary famously urged his disciples to "turn on, tune in, drop out." Another key individual who helped popularize LSD was the author Ken

MILITARY EXPERIMENTATION WITH LSD

During World War II, scientists working for the CIA began exploring the possibility of developing drugs that would break down a captive's psychological resistance during interrogations. As the Cold War began, the agency's goals became more ambitious. After LSD was synthesized, the drug seemed to have potential for inducing altered mental states that could make people easier to manipulate. Experimentation on human subjects began in 1951.

In 1953, the CIA launched MK-ULTRA, a research program that explored the use of drugs for mind-control purposes. Over the course of a decade, MK-ULTRA conducted and funded about 150 subprograms. Soldiers, psychiatric patients, prisoners, and ordinary members of the public were used as guinea pigs. Some of the experiments were ethical and legitimate, but many test subjects were given drugs without their knowledge. Later on, after details about MK-ULTRA were made public, some of the test subjects said that the experience had devastated their lives.

Kesey, who was introduced to the drug as a voluntary subject in the CIA's MK-ULTRA program. Kesey and a group of friends used LSD frequently as they traveled the country in a bus. Their adventures were described by the writer Tom Wolfe in *The Electric Kool-Aid Acid Test* (1968). Unlike Leary, Kesey did not attach much spiritual significance to LSD.

In 1963, LSD started to become widely available for purchase on the street. People began calling it "acid" and taking it for recreational purposes. Young people, especially, were drawn to LSD and other novel experiences. They began to consider themselves a counterculture that rejected their parents' values and lifestyles. LSD was one of the emblems of the movement, influencing the art, music, and mind-set of the 1960s.

The trend alarmed mainstream Americans, who were bewildered by the social and cultural transformations sweeping the nation. Many factors contributed to the rebellion, protest, and social changes of the 1960s. But to many people concerned about the direction in which society was heading, LSD was an obvious culprit and a very dangerous and destabilizing substance. In 1966, *Life* magazine featured as its cover story "LSD: The Exploding Threat of the Mind Drug That Got Out of Control."

Legitimate doctors and even visionaries such as Aldous Huxley were disturbed by young people's casual use and abuse of LSD. Young people were taking massive doses of the drug, often under chaotic circumstances that combined reckless behavior and the abuse of other intoxicating or mind-altering

Ken Kesey and his band of Merry Pranksters sit on top of the vividly painted former school bus called "Further" in New Mexico during their LSD-fueled escapades in 1969.

substances. Many became disillusioned and even traumatized by the excesses of the late 1960s. In 1968, LSD was made illegal, bringing the turbulent era of legal experimentation to a close.

A Short Trip

Rates of LSD use declined drastically after 1970. New drugs emerged to take LSD's place as the primary threat to social order in the public eye. One of these was Ecstasy, which became popular during the 1990s as part of the emerging rave scene. LSD use also resurged slightly during this time, but only temporarily.

The University of Michigan has undertaken an ongoing study of American youth, including their behaviors, attitudes, and values. Each year it releases a report, "Monitoring the Future." The report summarizes the results of questionnaires completed by eighth-, tenth-, and twelfth-grade students. In 2012, the "Monitoring the Future" survey found that only 3.8 percent of high school seniors had ever used LSD. By contrast, 45.2 percent had used marijuana and 4.9 percent had used cocaine. The average user is an adolescent or young adult white male. Rates of LSD use are very low among minorities. Typically, people experiment with LSD once or twice without ever becoming regular users. About 25 percent of high school seniors reported that LSD would be easy to obtain.

Today, LSD is usually sold as a sheet of blotter paper composed of many small tabs. These tabs are torn off and ingested. It is such a potent hallucinogen that doses are measured in micrograms. Most drugs are measured in milligrams—a thousandfold greater. Blotters are made by dipping the paper into a liquid solution, drying it, and perforating it into squares. The amount absorbed by each small square is enough for a dose. LSD can also be found in the form of microdots, sugar cubes, liquid, and gelatin squares.

2

FROM
MAGIC MUSHROOMS
TO
DESIGNER DRUGS

Human beings throughout the world have used hallucinogenic substances since prehistoric times. Archaeologists believe that cave art painted seven thousand to nine thousand years ago depicts hallucinogenic mushrooms. Traditional societies used hallucinogens ritually to induce visions. Some cultures continue such practices to this day.

In the early twentieth century, therapists and psychiatrists believed that hallucinogens had the potential to help the

An initiate ingests iboga during a ceremony in Gabon, Africa. The active agent in the plant is ibogaine, a potent stimulant and hallucinogen with prolonged effects similar to those of LSD.

mentally ill. Curiosity about the drugs spread to people interested in using mind-altering substances to induce mystical experiences and explore their own consciousness. Later on, hallucinogens became popular as recreational drugs.

Today, common hallucinogens comprise a range of substances far wider and potentially more dangerous than ever before. This inherent danger is compounded because recreational users often lack any basic knowledge of the drug they're ingesting. In the past, traditional shamans, therapists, and even psychedelic gurus were familiar with the properties, risks, safe dosages, and dangers of hallucinogens. They were often the only members of society to ingest the substances. A twenty-first-century teenager taking random pills at a wild party could be in for severe and lasting physical side effects and a traumatizing psychological experience.

Psilocybin

Psilocybin is the psychedelic agent in hallucinogenic mushrooms, most of which belong to the genus *Psilocybe*. They are often called "magic mushrooms" or "shrooms." Hallucinogenic mushrooms have been used in Native American rituals for thousands of years.

In the 1950s, as interest in hallucinogens spread, people began experimenting with psilocybin mushrooms. Eventually, Albert Hofmann (the same biochemist who synthesized LSD) extracted psilocybin and psilocyn, another psychedelic agent present in smaller amounts. Like LSD, psilocybin became popular during the 1960s. Its users hoped to undergo a transformative or spiritual experience by using the drug. Some of these users viewed psilocybin as a "natural" alternative to LSD. It was made illegal in 1968.

Psychedelic mushrooms contain less than .5 percent of psilocybin and only trace amounts of psilocyn. The strength varies greatly among different species of mushroom and even between individual specimens of the same species. A user's misidentification of the mushrooms is a real risk. *Psilocybe* mushrooms are not dangerously toxic, but hallucinogenic mushrooms of other genuses are poisonous and can even be fatal.

The mushrooms are typically consumed fresh or dried, and powdered dried mushrooms are sometimes brewed into a tea. Doses are generally about 4 to 10 milligrams, or two to five *Psylocybe cyanenscens* mushrooms. Although it is possible to create psilocybin synthetically, it is not readily available. Anything sold as synthetic psylocybin is probably some other substance.

Mescaline

Mescaline is the active compound in peyote and several other species of cactus native to Mexico and the southwestern United States. Like psilocybin, mescaline has long been used in Native American religious rites.

Peyote was the first hallucinogenic plant to be analyzed chemically. A German chemist named Arthur Heffter first isolated mescaline from dried peyote buttons in 1896. Synthetic mescaline was created in 1919. In the 1950s, psychiatrist Dr. Humphry Osmond studied mescaline while researching the effects of hallucinogens in Saskatchewan, Canada. Author Aldous Huxley wrote about using mescaline in his book *The Doors of Perception*.

In 1956, Native Canadians invited Osmond and two other mental health researchers to observe a peyote ceremony. They

A peyote cactus flowers in the Arizona desert. The slow-growing plant can live for over a hundred years, and buttons from a single cactus can be harvested repeatedly.

hoped to counter sensationalistic rumors about peyote use by the Native American Church. The three men concluded that peyote use was not harmful in this ceremonial context and should not be banned for Native American religious purposes.

Peyote and mescaline were made illegal in the United States in 1970—growing the cacti is also illegal—but federal law exempted use of peyote in religious ceremonies of the Native American Church. Many states also allow ceremonial use.

PEYOTE AND THE NATIVE AMERICAN CHURCH

Peyote is used in ceremonies by members of the Native American Church, which incorporates both Native American rituals and Christian practices. A group peyote ceremony traditionally extends throughout the night, with each person consuming buttons of peyote during a series of rounds. Sacramental use of peyote is protected by the First Amendment of the U.S. Constitution, which provides for freedom of religious practice. Only licensed members of the Native American Church can legally harvest peyote, even on private land.

Like many aspects of drug law, ceremonial peyote use has been the subject of controversy and shifting policy. The Comprehensive Drug Abuse Prevention and Control Act of 1970 exempted peyote use by the Native American Church. In 1979, however, a group of non-Native Americans proposed to organize a church that used peyote in rituals, and the attempt was struck down in a state court. In 1990, the U.S. Supreme Court upheld the legality of an Oregon state law prohibiting ceremonial use of peyote. In 1993, Congress passed the Religious Freedom Restoration Act (RFRA), which protected religious practices such as peyote use.

The U.S. Supreme Court overturned the Act in 1997. A lower court subsequently interpreted the issue more narrowly, ruling that the federal government must comply with the terms of the RFRA. As a result, laws covering ceremonial peyote use vary from one state to another.

A peyote cactus consists of one or more small spineless buttons and a long root. The buttons are sliced off and either consumed fresh or dried. Dried peyote contains about 1 to 5 percent mescaline by weight, and a dose consists of about three to twelve buttons. Users generally swallow buttons whole, though it can also be powdered or brewed into a tea. Pure mescaline is taken in powder form or as a capsule, tablet, or liquid. Mescaline is not a highly popular drug, in part because of the terrible taste of peyote buttons and the intense nausea that accompanies the experience.

Phencyclidine

Phencyclidine (PCP), sometimes called "angel dust," is a synthetic compound classified as a dissociative anesthetic. It is a highly complex drug that can induce effects of a stimulant, a depressant, and a hallucinogen. The specific effects depend on the dose, the means by which it is taken, and the circumstances under which it is taken.

First synthesized in 1926, PCP was marketed as an anesthetic in 1957. It was withdrawn in 1965 due to patients' bad reactions to the drug. These included delusions, extreme anxiety, paranoia, and even psychotic behavior. It was sold as a veterinary anesthetic from 1967 to 1978, when the drug was finally made illegal.

Pure PCP is a white powder, but it is also sold in the form of a tablet, capsule, or liquid. Users most often smoke PCP, sometimes by mixing it with tobacco or marijuana or

Containers of PCP are shown in a storage facility after a drug bust in Los Angeles, California. Over 100 gallons (379 liters) of the drug, worth over $100 million, were seized—enough to dose ten million people.

dipping cigarettes into liquid PCP. It can also be ingested, snorted, or injected. A low dose is under 5 mg; a high dose is over 10 mg. Dosage sizes are difficult to control because the purity of PCP varies from one sample to another. Since PCP is easy to manufacture, it is sometimes used to adulterate other illegal drugs. Because of its extreme and usually unpleasant effects, PCP is not a highly popular drug.

Ketamine

Ketamine, sometimes called "special K," is another dissociative anesthetic. Its effects, however, are less extreme than those of PCP (ketamine is often referred to as "cat tranquilizer," while PCP is nicknamed "elephant tranquilizer"). Ketamine, first synthesized in 1961, was first marketed as an anesthetic for both medical and veterinary purposes. Doctors still use ketamine on humans in some cases, such as for patients with cardiac problems that could be worsened by more commonly used anesthetics. Ketamine is also a safe and effective sedative for children, who don't experience the sometimes disturbing hallucinations that the drug causes in adults.

Since people sometimes take ketamine before partying, it is sometimes referred to as a club drug. Most illicit ketamine is stolen from medical or veterinary stock, which is packaged as a liquid. The liquid is sometimes dried, leaving behind a powder. Ketamine on the street is sold as a powder, tablet, or liquid. Used recreationally, it is usually snorted or ingested. Sometimes it is smoked or injected into the muscle.

Since ketamine is used for legitimate medical purposes, it is easier for researchers to study its effects than it is for some more tightly restricted drugs. Indeed, ketamine has shown promise as a treatment for depression, chronic pain, and extreme childhood fear.

Ecstasy

The synthetic drug 3,4-methylenedioxymethamphetamine (MDMA) is better known by its common name, Ecstasy. It is a designer drug. This means that it was never sold on the market by a pharmaceutical company for legitimate medical purposes. Ecstasy is not a traditional hallucinogen, although, like typical hallucinogens, it affects mood and perceptions. Since it induces increased empathy, it is sometimes classified as an empathogen or entactogen. The U.S. Food and Drug Administration (FDA) has never approved Ecstasy for any legit-imate medical or psychiatric uses.

Ecstasy was first synthesized in 1912 by the German phar-maceutical company Merck. It received little attention until 1978, when biochemist Alexander Shulgin published an article on its effects and possible applications in psychiatric therapy. Some psychotherapists began experimenting with the drug, hoping that it could help patients resolve their problems by promoting trust and openness during sessions. Some thera-pists tried the drug themselves, as well as administering it to their patients. These applications of Ecstasy were not scientific research trials, nor did they have any formal approval. In 1985, Ecstasy was made illegal due to formal trials that showed that the drug could produce brain damage in animals.

Nevertheless, illegal use of Ecstasy increased throughout the 1980s. During the 1990s, it was particularly popular for the energy, euphoria, and easing of social anxiety experienced by its

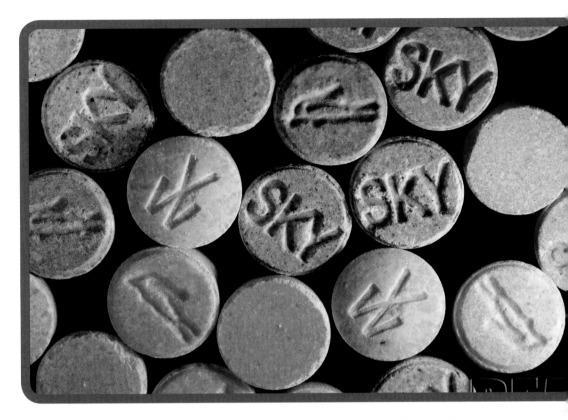

Ecstasy pills are often imprinted with logos. Most Ecstasy sold on the street is manufactured internationally in illegal labs, and it is usually not pure. In fact, many samples contain no MDMA at all.

users. Partiers tended to use it at raves and dance clubs, and use of Ecstasy soon spread to other social settings. According to the "Monitoring the Future" survey, rates of Ecstasy use peaked in 2001 and then fell in subsequent years. This decline is probably due to effective education campaigns on the drug's risks and unpleasant and sometimes dangerous side effects. In 2012, 3.8 percent of all twelfth graders had used Ecstasy in the past year.

Ecstasy is usually sold as a tablet and ingested, though it also comes in the form of powders or gel tabs. It is synthesized in illegal labs and is often adulterated with other substances. A single dose is between 80 and 120 mg.

Other Hallucinogens

A variety of lesser-known hallucinogens exist, both legal and illegal, naturally occurring and synthetic. DMT is a synthetic compound that induces highly vivid effects that dissipate in less than a half hour. Compounds related to DMT are found in many natural sources, including plants and the venom of a species of South American toad. Ayahuasca (also called yagé) is a brewed tea containing extracts from two different plants. One of the active agents in ayahuasca is DMT. Religious use of ayahuasca is permitted by the federal government.

Numerous plants that are native to North America contain hallucinogenic compounds. Just because they occur naturally, however, doesn't make them in the least bit safe—many of these plants are also highly toxic. An herb in the mint family called *Salvia divinorum* can induce psychedelic effects when chewed or smoked. Several plants contain belladonna alkaloids, which induce extreme and dangerous physical and mental effects. These plants include jimsonweed, deadly nightshade, and mandrake.

Many synthetic designer drugs have hallucinogenic or empathogenic properties, which are sometimes combined with the effects of stimulants or other categories of drug. Designer drugs are often derivatives of known compounds. They may have been originally synthesized by pharmaceutical companies but never used for legitimate medical purposes. In other cases, they are developed by independent chemists who want to make money on "legal" drugs that are too new to have yet been outlawed. The short-term and long-term effects of these untested drugs are unpredictable and potentially dangerous. There is no way for the buyer to know the composition or the dosage of a designer drug.

3

THE EFFECTS OF HALLUCINOGENS ON THE BRAIN AND BODY

Hallucinogens affect the user's senses, mood, and thoughts by changing the actions of neurotransmitters in the brain. Different drugs have different neurochemical mechanisms, and they vary in strength and effects on the brain and body. Hallucinogens consist of four different categories: psychedelics, dissociatives, empathogens, and deliriants.

The dangers also vary greatly among hallucinogens, and people are often unaware of the specific risks associated with any given drug. Most hallucinogens carry the danger of a "bad trip" negatively affecting the mind and mood. There is no antidote or quick fix for the psychological effects of a hallucinogen. If a person is taken to the hospital due to a reaction such as extreme agitation, the medical staff usually isolates the individual in a dim, quiet room where he or she is attended by a friend or family member. At most, hospital staff may administer a sedative. Only time brings the trip to an end; it's a waiting game. Adverse physical effects from hallucinogen overdoses, however, may require more active medical attention.

Many of the risks of hallucinogens are out of the user's control, but some factors can make a bad trip even worse. Large doses are a prescription for disaster. Someone who is fearful and expects to have a bad trip will almost certainly have one. Even those anticipating a blissful experience, however, can be surprised by something far more nightmarish, especially if they are in an unfamiliar environment and not surrounded by supportive and caring friends. Users of hallucinogens can be vulnerable to accidents or injury while impaired by the drug. People who use hallucinogens at parties or clubs may even be at risk of theft or assault. They may become so dazed, disoriented, and vulnerable by the drug that they become easy prey.

Psychedelics

LSD, psilocybin, and mescaline are the three hallucinogens most associated with psychedelic experiences. They work by affecting

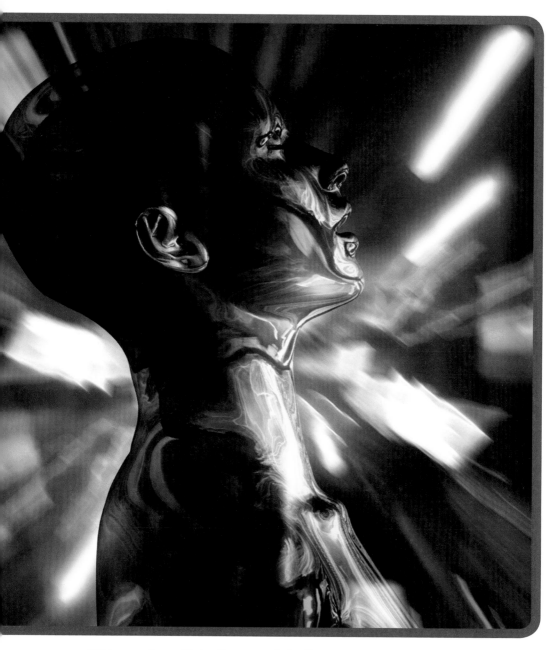

LSD has an extreme effect on the senses. As Dr. Albert Hofmann wrote of his first inadvertent trip, "I perceived an uninterrupted stream of fantastic pictures, extraordinary shapes with intense, kaleidoscopic play of colors."

the serotonin system in the brain. Serotonin is the neurotransmitter that helps regulate sleep, body temperature, appetite,
mood, muscle control, and sensory perception.

It is impossible to describe a "typical" experience using LSD
or other psychedelic hallucinogens because the effects vary
greatly. Two people taking the same dosage in the same setting
can have vastly different experiences. Results can vary for a
single individual from one use of the drug to another.

An LSD trip usually lasts for about twelve hours, peaking for
several hours midway through. Mild effects begin from about a
half hour to ninety minutes after taking the drug. Inexperienced
users sometimes take a second dose when the initial effects
are slow to occur. Since larger doses increase the effect—and
side effects—of the drug rather than its duration, this increases
the risks of a bad trip.

The primary psychological effects of LSD involve the emotions and senses. Sights and sounds become altered and
intensified, sometimes becoming overwhelming. Colors, light,
physical shapes, movements, self-image, and one's sense of time
grow distorted. People sometimes experience synesthesia—a
crossing of the different senses, such as "seeing" sounds and
"tasting" color.

The effects of LSD on the mood and emotions are what
can lead to a "bad trip." LSD diminishes people's control over
their emotional reactions. Some people feel uplifted and have
a spiritual or self-reflective experience. For others, the effects
on mood and emotion, combined with sensory overload, can

LSD distorts sensory perceptions, thoughts, and emotions. Some say they gain personal insight from the experience, but there is always a danger of the traumatizing "bad trip."

become overwhelming. The user may experience mood swings, loss of control, fear, delusions, despair, anxiety, and panic. In the worst-case scenario, a user may experience extreme anxiety or a psychotic reaction.

LSD causes minimal physical side effects, which can be uncomfortable but usually not dangerous. A typical dose ranges from 20 to 100 mg. It would take 14,000 mg—an almost impossibly large amount—to induce fatal physical symptoms. Physical effects include nausea, aches, blurred vision, and increased body temperature.

Users often feel fatigued and drained the day after using the drug. Psychological aftereffects may persist for days and even weeks. Some people are left feeling disturbed or even traumatized. A user can quickly develop a tolerance to LSD, meaning that larger doses will be required to achieve the same effect if the drug is used frequently. An LSD trip is such a draining experience, however, that even habitual users take the drug less than once a month or, at most, once a week. A cross-tolerance also exists among LSD, psilocybin, and mescaline—anyone who uses one of the drugs develops a tolerance to the effects of all three.

Psilocybin produces effects similar to those of LSD. The experience is much shorter—lasting about six hours—and some people find it milder than LSD. As with LSD, there are few physical dangers to using psilocybin, although users may feel nauseous or drowsy. These effects increase with dosage.

The chemical properties of mescaline are different from those of LSD and psilocybin, although the psychological experience is similar. The effects last for about ten hours. The experience of taking pure mescaline is slightly different from ingesting a cactus button, since the plant contains other active agents in addition to mescaline. Some of the physical effects of mescaline resemble those of stimulants, such as increased heart rate and blood pressure.

Dissociatives

Dissociative anesthetics, which include PCP and ketamine, create a psychological effect of detachment from the environment and from oneself. PCP users often retain no memories of their experience under the drug. Ketamine users sometimes refer to "going down the k-hole" on high doses of the drug, describing the effect as an out-of-body or near-death experience.

Dissociative anesthetics affect the actions of a neurotransmitter in the brain called glutamate that affects cognitive, motor, and sensory functions. Users on dissociative anesthetics lose coordination and may appear to be in a stupor. *Salvia divinorum* and the cough medicine ingredient DXM also work as dissociative anesthetics.

PCP is a highly unpredictable drug, often causing agitation, delusions, panic, and psychotic or violent behavior. Users can experience intense hallucinations and a feeling of invulnerability. PCP also acts as a stimulant and painkiller. The length of an episode depends on the means of taking the drug, but it typically lasts from four to six hours, with aftereffects lingering for much longer.

The effects of ketamine are similar to those of PCP, although milder and less disturbing. Users experience hallucinations and may feel like they're floating. The experience can sometimes resemble a dreamlike state or trance. The effects usually last from forty-five to ninety minutes.

The physical effects caused by PCP and ketamine are the most dangerous of any hallucinogen. Unpleasant side effects can include nausea, loss of balance, and numbness of the hands and feet. At high doses, physical symptoms can be drastic and potentially life threatening. Users who overdose can experience shallow breathing, high blood pressure, convulsions, and a state of coma. Dissociative anesthetics are particularly dangerous to mix with alcohol or sedatives.

PCP and ketamine are both addictive. They are not physically addictive, but users can form psychological dependencies on the drugs.

Empathogens

The terms "empathogen" and "entactogen" describe drugs that produce feelings of empathy and social openness. Their properties fall somewhere between those of stimulants and hallucinogens. Ecstasy and many other designer drugs act as empathogens. Ecstasy works its effects on the emotions by increasing the levels of the neurotransmitter serotonin in the brain, although scientists don't fully understand the drug's mechanism.

Ecstasy often creates feelings of intimacy toward others, relaxation, heightened sensations, and a general sense of

Ecstasy is popular as a club drug. Yet thousands of deaths have resulted from the dehydration associated with elevated body temperature and from contaminated tablets.

well-being. It may also diminish negative emotions such as fear and aggression. Ecstasy is sometimes called the "hug drug." Users generally do not experience hallucinations or bad trips. The effects of Ecstasy last for three to five hours, peaking around the midpoint.

Physically, people feel energized and exhilarated—Ecstasy is popular at all-night dance parties. Other physical effects are unpleasant and potentially dangerous, including nausea, muscle tension, and faintness. Users also tend to feel jittery and clench their jaw. Ecstasy interferes with the body's ability to regulate temperature, which can lead to overheating and dehydration. Other stimulant effects include increased heart rate and blood pressure. It is possible to lethally overdose on Ecstasy. In addition, the drug is often adulterated with other substances that could pose additional risks.

The unpleasant aftereffects of Ecstasy can linger for days. The user often feels fatigued, emotionally drained, anxious, and depressed. Some studies have shown that Ecstasy may cause long-lasting changes in the brain. Frequent users of Ecstasy can develop a tolerance to the drug that requires them to take ever larger doses in order to feel any effect.

Deliriants

Deliriants are a class of drug that induces an extreme sense of disorientation accompanied by hallucinations. The most potent deliriants are belladonna alkaloids found in plants, including deadly nightshade, mandrake, henbane, and datura (which includes jimsonweed). These plants have a long history of medicinal and ritual use. They were used by medieval witches and poisoners alike.

Belladonna alkaloids work by affecting part of the brain's nervous system. They cause physical symptoms such as dry mouth and skin, increased body temperature, dilated pupils, and increased heart rate. One of the nerve receptors responsible

JIMSONWEED

Abuse of some drugs might lead to a stint in rehab. Abuse of jimsonweed, however, is more likely to require recuperation in the intensive care unit of the hospital. A plant commonly found in the wild and cultivated in flowerbeds, jimsonweed contains the chemical agents atropine and scopolamine. Every part of the plant is poisonous and potentially deadly, especially the seeds.

Jimsonweed produces hallucinations and extreme physical symptoms. The effects are summed up in the ditty, "Red as a beet, blind as a bat, dry as a bone, mad as a hatter, hotter than hellfire."

Jimsonweed produces a state of delirium accompanied by intense hallucinations, often followed by amnesia of the episode. The chemical agents in jimsonweed also cause drastic physical symptoms, including racing heart rate, rapid breathing, increased body temperature, and dilated pupils. The aftereffects of jimsonweed can linger for days or even longer. Large doses can lead to convulsions, coma, and even death.

Jimsonweed is most often used by teenagers who are ignorant or dismissive of the dangers. They sometimes believe erroneously that the effects are similar to those of marijuana. In other cases, people have eaten jimsonweed after mistaking it for an edible herb.

for the effects is also stimulated by nicotine, the active agent in tobacco.

People who use deliriants often experience a bizarre and unpleasant dream state followed by amnesia. Belladonna alkaloids produce genuine hallucinations, rather than the visual distortions caused by psychedelics such as LSD. As a result of this break from reality, users may lose control of their own actions. Deliriants are not widely used because of users' typically bad experiences and severe physical side effects.

4

GETTING HELP

For some people, it may seem inexplicable that anyone would voluntarily dose themselves with a dangerous, illegal substance capable of damaging the brain and body. People choose to take drugs for a variety of reasons. They might be looking for a fun time, a euphoric experience, or a distraction from daily cares and stresses. They may just want to try something new—young adults in particular tend to seek out novel experiences. A user may choose to experiment with hallucinogens in particular because of their reputation for expanding one's consciousness and leading to spiritual or cosmic insights.

Many people who casually use hallucinogens never experience drastic side effects. Others, however, can have their lives negatively impacted by hallucinogen use. In particular, people who have a tendency toward or a family history of addiction or mental illness may be vulnerable to the potential risks of the drugs.

Abuse, Addiction, Treatment, and Recovery

Most hallucinogens are not addictive. PCP and ketamine, however, can create a psychological dependency. Ecstasy may also have some potential for psychological addiction. Drug users may also use hallucinogens as a means of escaping from the realities of their lives. Poly-drug abusers or addicts may use hallucinogens in addition to other types of drugs.

Substance abuse is the use of an illicit substance or the misuse of a legal substance such as alcohol or prescription drugs. Abuse can lead to addiction, in which the user feels that he or she is compelled to use a substance regardless of negative consequences. Addiction is a disease that affects how a person's brain functions. Effective treatment programs use medical principles to help addicts stop their abuse of drugs.

The first step toward recovery from a drug addiction is recognizing the problem. Drug addicts are unable to control their need for the drug. They develop a tolerance to it and must use larger and larger amounts to achieve the same effect. Even when

Chronic drug use can take a toll on daily activities, affecting performance in school, work, and relationships.

drug use is no longer a source of pleasure, an addict must continue using the substance just to avoid feeling poorly. Drug abuse may take a heavy toll on work, school, family relations, and social life, but the addict continues to seek and use the drug despite the negative consequences. In some cases, family or friends may have to stage an intervention before a drug addict will seek treatment.

Drug treatment involves multiple components that address different aspects of an individual's addiction. There is no one-size-fits-all plan. Many addicts take part in various types of therapy, such as behavioral therapy, group therapy, or family therapy. Some addicts

FLASHBACKS

Users of LSD, psilocybin, mescaline, and many other hallucinogens may experience flashbacks, sometimes called posthallucinogen perceptual disorder, long after using the drug. Flashbacks are sudden brief recurrences of hallucinogenic effects. They usually involve visual distortions related to a previous LSD trip and are sometimes accompanied by physical sensations or shifts in mood. Flashbacks are most likely to occur when someone is stressed, tired, or using alcohol or drugs such as marijuana. Antidepressants such as Prozac may also trigger flashbacks.

Heavy hallucinogen users and people with mental disorders are more likely to experience flashbacks. Occurrences are impossible to predict, though—it is even possible for one-time users to experience flashbacks. Episodes generally diminish in the months following hallucinogen use, but some people experience flashbacks for years afterward. In extreme cases, which are diagnosed as hallucinogen persisting perception disorder (HPPD), flashbacks can be reoccurring and disturbing.

receive medication. An effective treatment plan also addresses other issues that are essential to recovery, such as medical and psychological problems.

An addict is recovered once he or she can return to the normal, drug-free routines of work, social, and family life. Drug addiction is a chronic disease, and recovery can be a long-term struggle. Self-help groups such as twelve-step programs can help support a recovering addict.

Resources such as twelve-step programs sometimes offer housing and other forms of support to recovering drug users trying to maintain a substance-free lifestyle.

Drug Use and Mental Illness

Substance abuse and mental illness tend to be connected. People with mental illness may be more susceptible to substance abuse, while substance abuse can exacerbate pre-existing mental illness. Individuals with mental illness may self-medicate by turning to drugs and alcohol in an attempt to alleviate feelings of anxiety or depression. Such behavior may temporarily numb the symptoms, but, over the long term, it can make mental health problems even worse. The risks may be even higher for

One repeated claim is that LSD can make people go insane, specifically by causing long-term psychosis. No research has proven that LSD directly leads to long-term psychiatric problems. Yet, it can trigger or worsen mental illness in those predisposed to it.

young adults, since the teenage brain is still developing and some substances work differently on children's or adolescents' brains than on the adult brain.

Hallucinogens—particularly LSD and PCP—may trigger symptoms of conditions such as schizophrenia or bipolar disorder in people who already have a predisposition to or family history of mental illness. This is because the effects of hallucinogens closely resemble the psychotic symptoms of these conditions. Psychosis is marked by a break with reality that may involve delusions and hallucinations. Essentially, hallucinogens probably do not make people psychotic or mentally ill, but they may unmask underlying and pre-existing psychological problems.

According to the National Institutes of Health (NIH), as many as six in ten people with substance abuse problems also suffer from another mental illness. A relapse in either condition frequently triggers a decline in the other. Some doctors believe that substance abuse and mental illness might be different aspects of a single disease. The most successful treatment programs address both mental health and substance abuse issues.

MYTHS & FACTS

MYTH LSD damages the chromosomes.

FACT A controversial 1967 study reported that LSD damaged white blood cell chromosomes in the lab. However, further research found no evidence that LSD caused mutations in chromosomes.

MYTH A drug described as a "legal high" is safe to use.

FACT Many synthetic designer drugs advertised as "legal highs" have not yet been evaluated by the FDA. Some designer drugs produce both stimulant and hallucinogenic effects, which can involve risky psychological and physical side effects.

MYTH Hallucinogenic mushrooms can be poisonous.

FACT Psilocybin mushrooms are not poisonous. They should not be confused with *Amanita muscaria*, a toxic mushroom that acts as a deliriant. Users who consume *A. muscaria* experience hallucinations, as well as nausea, increased heart rate, and other physical effects that may require hospitalization.

CHAPTER 5

HALLUCINOGENS
AND THE
LAW

For most of U.S. history, few laws restricted or regulated drugs, either legal or illegal. The first significant law, passed in 1906, required that only patent medicines include a list of ingredients. Over the next sixty years, a patchwork of laws and amendments were enacted that prohibited or controlled various drugs.

The drug use and rebellious spirit of the 1960s alarmed many lawmakers. President Lyndon B. Johnson singled out LSD as a particular threat to society in his 1968 State of the Union address. That same year, his first proposed bill outlawed hallucinogens.

In 1970, the government passed the Comprehensive Drug Abuse Prevention and Control Act. It consolidated drug laws and classified drugs by their medical value, danger, and potential for abuse. From 1970 to 2000, the rates of imprisonment for drug offenses increased more than fivefold. The 1970 act, enforced by the FDA and the Drug Enforcement Administration (DEA), remains the legal foundation for U.S. drug policy.

Controlled Substances

The Controlled Substances Act, part of the Comprehensive Drug Abuse Prevention and Control Act of 1970, categorizes drugs into five levels of control. The most stringent level is Schedule I, which includes drugs considered to have a very high potential for abuse and no accepted medical use. LSD, DMT, mescaline, peyote, psilocybin, and psilocyn were listed as Schedule I drugs when the act was passed.

Ecstasy became a drug of concern as recreational use increased during the 1980s. Despite lawmakers' condemnation of the drug, some therapists argued that Ecstasy possessed medical value and that the drug's risks were manageable. In 1985, the DEA's emergency scheduling authority listed Ecstasy as a Schedule I drug for a year. Subsequently, a DEA law judge recommended that Ecstasy be placed permanently under

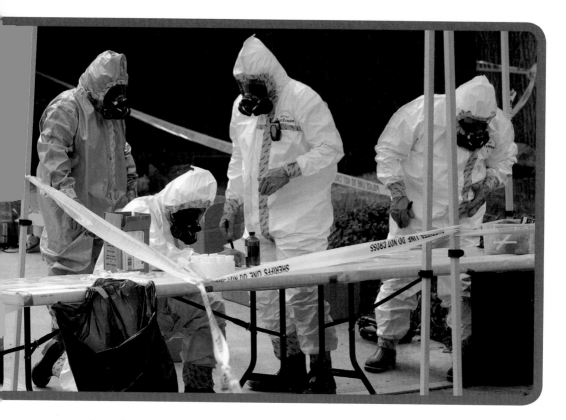

Law enforcement technicians test evidence seized from a home in Boulder, Colorado, where the residents were suspected of operating an illegal Ecstasy-producing lab.

Schedule III. This category includes drugs with high abuse potential but accepted medical use. Schedule III drugs can be prescribed by a doctor. Despite the judge's recommendation, however, the DEA listed Ecstasy as a Schedule I drug in 1988.

Schedule II drugs are considered to have a very high abuse potential and accepted medical use, though they are strictly regulated. PCP is classified as a Schedule II drug.

A drug is classified as a controlled substance when evidence indicates that it has become subject to abuse and could harm

ALEXANDER SHULGIN AND THE 2C DRUGS

Alexander Shulgin (1925–) is a biochemist and researcher sometimes called the "Godfather of Ecstasy." During the 1960s, Shulgin became convinced that psychoactive drugs could have psychological benefits. In 1976, he began promoting the little-known drug Ecstasy as an aid for helping patients share their feelings during therapy sessions.

Shulgin also synthesized and experimented with nearly two hundred hallucinogenic compounds. Many have unique effects on the senses and mood. For two decades, Shulgin held a research license for handling Schedule I drugs. Once created, however, Shulgin's drugs often proved dangerous to users and were declared illegal.

One of Shulgin's discoveries was the 2C series of psychoactive drugs, which have a chemical structure similar to Ecstasy. They tend to create an agitated state of euphoria and delirium. Unlike LSD and psilocybin, 2C drugs can have dangerous physical effects, including increased body temperature, elevated heart rate, and seizures. In some cases, people have died after taking 2C drugs.

2C drugs are often sold with the claim that they're legal, which misleads users into believing that they are safe. As with any designer drug synthesized in an illegal lab, there is no way of knowing the composition or strength of the compound. In 2012, the drug 2C-I, or "smiles," was linked to the deaths of two teenagers. Police warned the public about a tainted batch of the drug in circulation.

users. Ketamine, for example, was classified as Schedule III in 1999 due to a rise in abuse of the drug. Precursor chemicals to illegal drugs are also listed as controlled substances. Lysergic acid, for example, is categorized as a Schedule III drug. It does not have any potential for abuse, but it can be used to manufacture LSD.

New designer drugs pose significant difficulties for the legal system. Often these chemicals produce effects similar to those of LSD, Ecstasy, or other drugs, but they differ very slightly in molecular structure. Therefore, they are technically legal until studied and classified by the DEA, a time-consuming process. With new designer drugs proliferating—hundreds enter the market every year—investigators and scientists have trouble keeping up.

Legal Consequences

Under the Comprehensive Drug Abuse Prevention and Control Act, penalties for drug offenses were significantly increased. Since then, various presidential administrations have declared war on drugs and imposed even more rigorous punishments for drug crimes. Laws vary depending on the jurisdiction—federal or state, juvenile or adult court, for example—and they tend to change from one year to another.

A person caught holding drugs may be charged with possession, distribution, or manufacturing. Possession of smaller amounts of drugs generally results in misdemeanor charges; larger amounts lead to the much more serious felony charges. Possession of a certain amount of a drug can result in an

A judge congratulates a drug offender—a military veteran suffering from mental health issues—on completing a program that combines treatment for both drug abuse and mental illness.

"intent to distribute" charge, regardless of the person's actual intent. Someone who associates with another person holding drugs can also receive a drug conspiracy charge—by lending a friend a car, for example—regardless of whether he or she even had contact with the drug.

First-time offenders usually receive more lenient penalties than repeat offenders. Certain offenses may require mandatory minimum sentences, meaning that a judge can't give an offender a lighter sentence based on the circumstances. He or she is forced to impose the minimum penalty, which is usually jail time for a significant period of time.

Medical Possibilities

After the passage of the Controlled Substances Act, research on LSD and other banned hallucinogens ceased from 1970 through the 2000s. In the late 2000s, however, researchers began proposing new research trials involving hallucinogens. In 2009, the FDA approved a Harvard clinical trial evaluating whether LSD could relieve anxiety in cancer patients—the first LSD research permitted in about fifty years. Other recent research has examined effects of psilocybin and Ecstasy.

Some of the new trials are revisiting the results of studies from the early days of LSD clinical research. Much of the older research does not meet modern standards, but it does identify intriguing possibilities for future inquiry. A study at Johns Hopkins examined whether psilocybin could help treat chronic addiction. Several studies have shown that psychedelic halluci- nogens can help people with conditions such as depression, anxiety, obsessive-compulsive disorder, and severe cluster head- aches. Ketamine has also shown potential for treating depression. Most of these studies are ongoing, and no definitive findings have been yet reviewed and approved.

Positive clinical results do not mean that hallucinogens will be approved for medical use anytime soon. Much more

Current research studies are examining whether or not psilocybin relieves anxiety in cancer patients. The pill shown here could contain psilocybin or it could be a placebo administered to a control group of patients.

research would be needed to evaluate the safety of the drugs and the appropriate circumstances and procedures for administering hallucinogens therapeutically. For example, Ecstasy has shown promise in treating post-traumatic stress disorder (PTSD), which can severely affect the daily lives of sufferers.

Nevertheless, Ecstasy use involves potential side effects, aftereffects, and possible long-term harm to the brain. Before it could be proposed as an effective treatment, much more research would have to be done on whether the benefits are worth the risks. Even if it was proved to be safe in some conditions, approval would still be unlikely, since policy makers are seldom willing to relax restrictions on illegal drugs.

TEN GREAT QUESTIONS TO ASK A DRUG COUNSELOR

1. What are the side effects that accompany the use of hallucinogenic drugs?

2. Do hallucinogenic drugs really induce mystical experiences or bad trips?

3. Do hallucinogenic drugs cause flashbacks?

4. What are the physical risks of taking LSD, PCP, ketamine, and Ecstasy?

5. Is Ecstasy often adulterated with other drugs and chemicals?

6. Is it possible to overdose on hallucinogens?

7. What are the warning signs of a substance abuse problem?

8. Has research shown hallucinogens to have any potential medical value?

9. Have there been any reports of designer drugs being sold in my town?

10. What are the penalties for possession of various types of hallucinogens in my state?

GLOSSARY

anesthetic A substance that causes insensitivity to pain.

cross-tolerance A condition in which tolerance of one drug lessens the response to another drug.

deliriant A drug that induces an extreme sense of disorientation, often accompanied by hallucinations and physical symptoms.

depressant A drug that relieves anxiety and slows physical reactions and activity.

Ecstasy MDMA; a type of illegal drug that induces hallucinogenic as well as stimulant effects.

mescaline A psychedelic agent extracted from the peyote cactus.

neurotransmitter A chemical that carries messages in the brain.

PCP Phencyclidine; a drug that acts as a dissociative anesthetic.

psilocybin A psychedelic agent extracted from a type of mushroom.

psychedelic Characterized by altered perceptions, thoughts, and emotions.

receptor A site in the nervous system that is affected by neurotransmitters or drug molecules.

serotonin A neurotransmitter that regulates functions such as body temperature, mood, and sensory perception.

stimulant A class of drugs that elevates mood and increases energy and alertness.

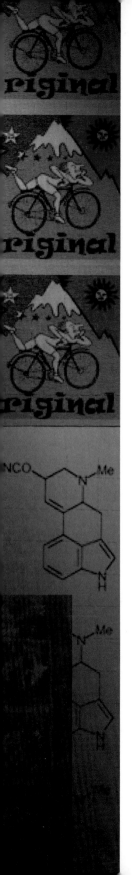

FOR MORE INFORMATION

Canadian Centre on Drug Abuse
75 Albert Street, Suite 500
Ottawa, ON K1P 5E7
Canada
(613) 235-4048
Web site: http://www.ccsa.ca
The Centre on Drug Abuse works to reduce
    alcohol- and drug-related harm.

Drug Policy Alliance
131 West 33rd Street, 15th Floor
New York, NY 10001
(212) 613-8020
Web site: http://www.drugpolicy.org
The Drug Policy Alliance aims to advance policies
    and attitudes that best reduce the harm of both
    drug use and drug prohibition.

Web Sites

Due to the changing nature of Internet links,
    Rosen Publishing has developed an online
    list of Web sites related to the subject of this
    book. This site is updated regularly. Please use
    this link to access the list:

http://www.rosenlinks.com/DAC/LSD

FOR FURTHER READING

Kramer, Ann. *Teen FAQ: Drugs*. Mankato, MN:
  Franklin Watts, 2010.

Kuhar, Michael. *The Addicted Brain: Why We
  Abuse Drugs, Alcohol, and Nicotine*. Upper
  Saddle River, NJ: FT Press, 2011.

Magill, Elizabeth, ed. *Drug Information for Teens*. 3rd
  ed. Detroit, MI: Omnigraphics, 2011.

Pilcher, Tim. *e, the incredibly strange history of
  ecstasy*. Philadelphia, PA: Running Press, 2008.

Santella, Thomas. *Hallucinogens*. New York, NY:
  Chelsea House Publishers, 2012.

Sheff, Nic. *We All Fall Down: Living with Addiction*.
  New York, NY: Little, Brown, 2011.

BIBLIOGRAPHY

Dyck, Erica. *Psychedelic Psychiatry: LSD from Clinic
  to Campus*. Baltimore, MD: Johns Hopkins
  University Press, 2008.

Gahlinger, Paul. *Illegal Drugs: A Complete Guide to
  Their History, Chemistry, Use, and Abuse*. New
  York, NY: Plume, 2004.

Kuhn, Cynthia, et. al. *Buzzed: The Straight Facts
  About the Most Used and Abused Drugs from
  Alcohol to Ecstasy*. New York, NY: W. W.
  Norton & Company, 2008.

Lee, Martin A., and Bruce Shlain. *Acid Dreams: The
  Complete Social History of LSD: The CIA, the Sixties,
  and Beyond*. New York, NY: Grove Press, 1992.

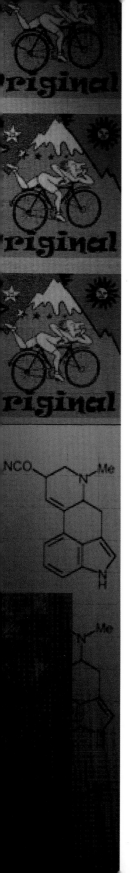

INDEX

About the Author

Corona Brezina has written over a dozen young adult books for Rosen Publishing. Several of her previous books have also focused on health and legal issues concerning teens, including *Teen Stress and Anxiety* and *FAQ Teen Life: Frequently Asked Questions About Juvenile Detention*. She lives in Chicago, Illinois.

Photo Credits

Cover, pp. 1, 27 U.S. DEA; pp. 4–5 Custom Medical Stock Photo; pp. 7, 17, 30, 42, 50, 59, 60, 62, 63, 64, 66 AFP/Getty Images; pp. 9, 11, 57 © AP Images; p. 15 © Lisa Law/The Image Works; p. 18 Photononstop/SuperStock; p. 21 Wild Horizon/Universal Images Group/Getty Images; p. 24 LA Impact/AP Images; p. 32 © iStockphoto.com/Perttu Sironen; p. 34 © iStockphoto.com/Ragip Candan; p. 38 © Luke Peters/Alamy; p. 40 Sam Abell/National Geographic Image Collection/Getty Images; pp. 44, 47 iStockphoto.com/Thinkstock; p. 46 Boston Globe/Getty Images; p. 52 Kathryn Scott Osler/Denver Post/Getty Images; p. 55 Christian Science Monitor/Getty Images.

Designer: Sam Zavieh; Photo Researcher: Amy Feinberg

Published in 2014 by The Rosen Publishing Group, Inc.
29 East 21st Street, New York, NY 10010

Library of Congress Cataloging-in-Publication Data

Brezina, Corona.
The truth about LSD and hallucinogens/Corona Brezina. — First edition.
   pages cm. — (Drugs & consequences)
Includes bibliographical references and index.
ISBN 978-1-4777-1901-5 (library binding)
1. LSD (Drug). 2. Hallucinogenic drugs. 3. Drug abuse. I. Title.
RM666.L88B74 2014
613.8'3—dc23

                                                      2013019266

Manufactured in the United States of America

CPSIA Compliance Information: Batch #W14YA: For further information, contact Rosen Publishing, New
York, New York, at 1-800-237-9932.

DRUGS & CONSEQUENCES

THE TRUTH ABOUT
LSD AND HALLUCINOGENS

PORTER COUNTY PUBLIC LIBRARY

CORONA BREZINA

ROSEN
PUBLISHING

New York